JOKES FOR 9 YEAR OLDS

FROM..................

Why did the woman put her money in the freezer?

a. *So she could have cold hard cash!*

Knock knock.
Who's there?
Beef.
Beef who?
Beef-ore you come in, please wipe your feet.

What do polar bears eat at cookouts?

a. Brrr-grrrs.

What do you get when there's an earthquake on the dairy farm?

a. A milkshake!

Knock knock.
Who's there?
Taco.
Taco who?
Taco-bout slow! What's taking so long?

Where do baby cows eat?

a. In the calfeteria!

How do dolphins decide who goes first in a football game?

a. They flipper a coin.

Knock knock.
Who's there?
Figs.
Figs who?
Figs the doorknob, it won't open!

What did the snowman ride to work?

a. His icycle!

Knock knock.
Who's there?
Lettuce.
Lettuce who?
Lettuce in, please, we've been waiting for hours!

When should you buy a boat?

a. When it's on sail!

What's it called when a snowman ignores his girlfriend?

a. Giving the cold shoulder.

What grants your wishes and helps get your car across the river?

a. *Your ferry godmother.*

What do polar bears make salads with?

a. *Iceberg lettuce.*

Knock knock.
Who's there?
Turnip.
Turnip who?
Turnip the volume, I can't hear!

How do birds pull nails out of wood?

a. With crowbars!

Knock knock.
Who's there?
Ada.
Ado who?
Ada delicious lunch, but now I'm here – let me in!

Why did the man eat the lamp?

a. He wanted a light snack.

What do skunks sing at Christmas?

a. *"Jingle Smells."*

Knock knock.
Who's there?
Alex.
Alex who?
Alex-plain later, alright?

Why did the man bring soda and ice cream on the raft?

a. *Because he wanted a root beer float!*

Knock knock.
Who's there?
Amanda.
Amanda who?
Amanda sell you something!

Why didn't the door open?

a. *Because it was knocked out!*

What time was it when the hippo sat on the clock?

a. *Time to get a new clock*

Why was the librarian in the garden?

a. He was weeding books!

What do you call a babbling cow?

Udder nonsense.

Knock knock.
Who's there?
Amy.
Amy who?
Amy-fraid I can't tell you!

Why did the window cry?

a. Because it had a pane!

Knock knock.
Who's there?
Anita.
Anita who?
Anita borrow an egg!

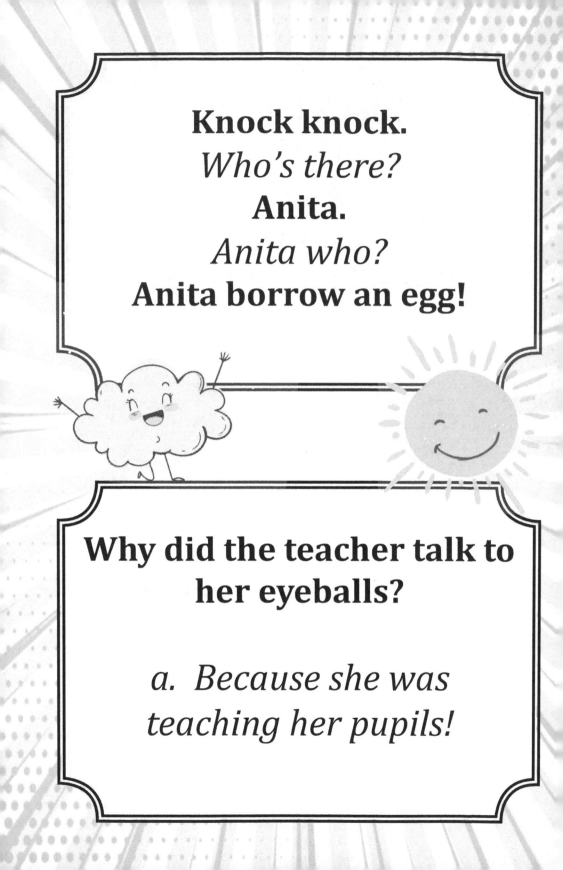

Why did the teacher talk to her eyeballs?

a. Because she was teaching her pupils!

How do octopi make squids laugh?

a. With ten tickles.

Knock knock.
Who's there?
Annie.
Annie who?
Annie-body home?

What would you get if you crossed a T-rex with a pig?

a. *Jurassic Pork.*

Knock knock.
Who's there?
Barbie.
Barbie who?
Barbie Q sauce!

What is the smallest room in the world?

a. A mushroom.

Why was the beekeeper's hair so sticky?

a. Because he used a honeycomb.

Why did the owl make everyone laugh?

a. Because he was a hoot!

Why did everyone love the snowman?

a. Because he was such an ice guy!

Knock knock.
Who's there?
Ben.
Ben who?
Ben waiting for half an hour, let me in already!

Why can you buy so many chicks at the store?

a. Because they're so cheep!

Knock knock.
Who's there?
Caesar.
Caesar who?
Caesar before she gets away!

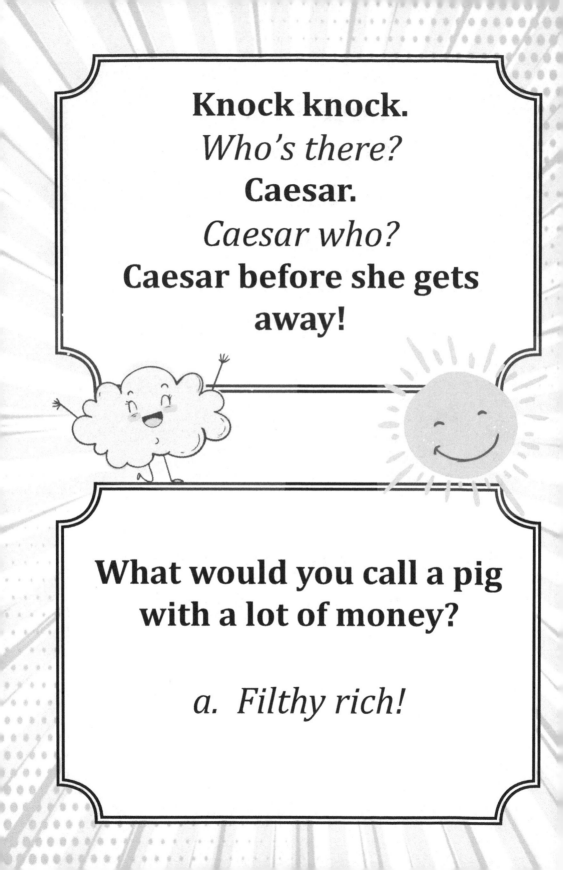

What would you call a pig with a lot of money?

a. Filthy rich!

Where does Dracula keep all his money?

a. At the blood bank!

What kind of button is always on you?

a. Your bellybutton!

Knock knock.
Who's there?
Candice.
Candice who?
Candice day get any weirder?

What do you say to a boot that keeps bothering you?

a. "Shoe!"

What did the outfielder say to the baseball?

a. *"Catch you later!"*

Knock knock.
Who's there?
Doris.
Doris who?
Doris still not opening, what's taking so long?

Where would you find a dog without any legs?

a. Right where you left it!

Knock knock.
Who's there?
Ash.
Ash who?
God bless you!

What small insect would you find on a clock?

a.   A tick.

How do trains eat their food?

a. They chew chew chew!

What part of your shirt uses the phone the most?

a. *Your caller.*

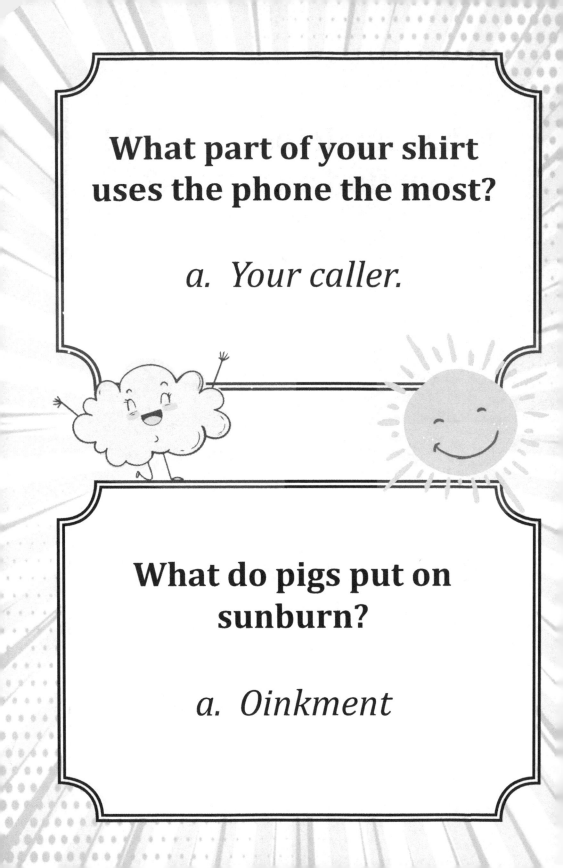

What do pigs put on sunburn?

a. *Oinkment*

Knock knock.
Who's there?
Amish.
Amish who?
Amish you, I can't wait to see you!

What did the man put on when his child was too bright?

a. Songlasses.

What do you call a dolphin accident?

a. Not on porpoise.

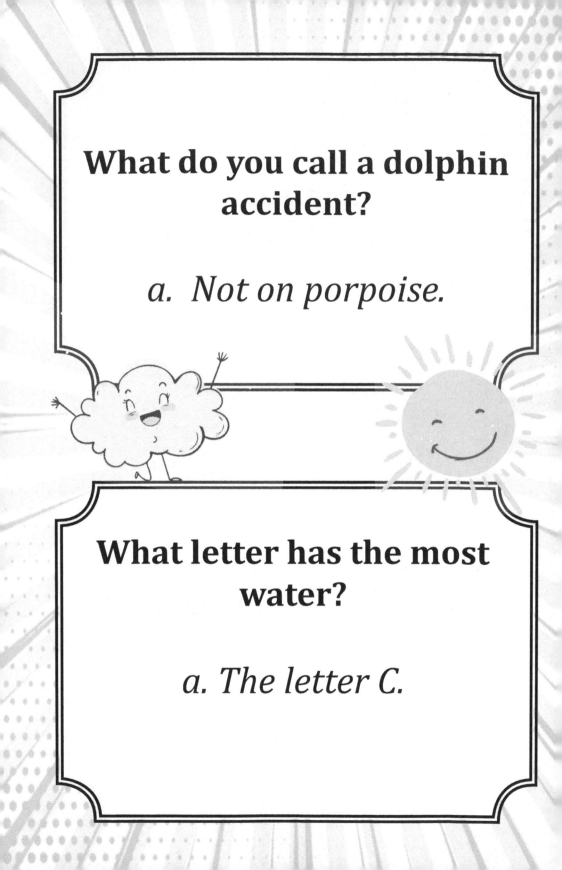

What letter has the most water?

a. The letter C.

Knock knock.
Who's there?
Venice.
Venice who?
Venice the rest of your family getting here?

What happened when the man was hit in the head by a snowball?

a. He was knocked out cold.

Knock knock.
Who's there?
Kenya.
Kenya who?
Kenya please let me inside?

What do eggs do when they hear funny jokes?

a. They crack up!

What did the keyboard say to the pencil?

a. "Sorry, you're not my type."

Knock knock.
Who's there?
Ida.
Ida who?
Ida-cline to answer until you open the door.

What does a candle do in the morning?

a. It wax up!

Knock knock.
Who's there?
Interrupting dog.
*Interrupting do-***WOOF WOOF WOOF!**

What season do math teachers love best?

a. Summer.

Why did the chicken cross the carnival?

a. To get to the other ride!

What do mountains wear to baseball games?

a. Ice caps.

What kind of shoes do ninjas wear?

a. Sneakers.

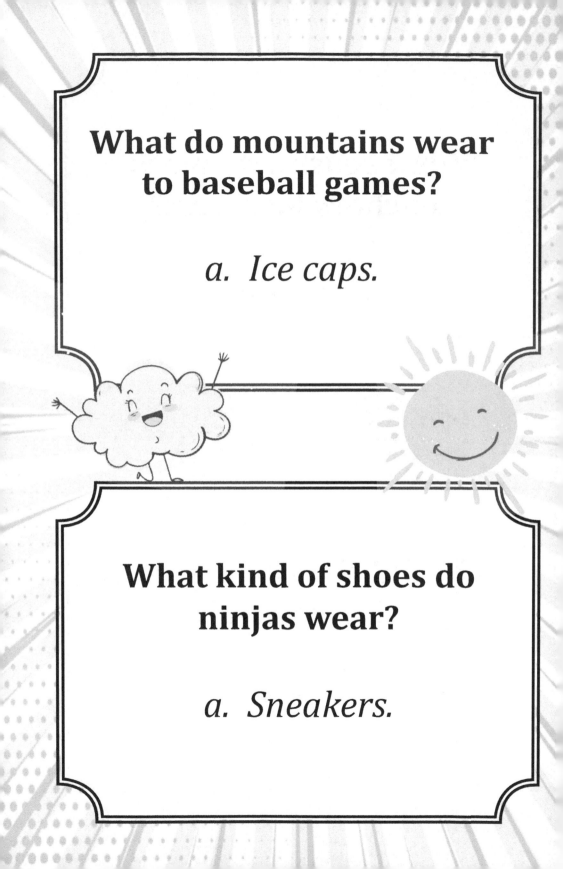

Knock knock.
Who's there?
Goat.
Goat who?
Goat tell your mom I'm here!

What happens when rabbits get married?

a. *They live hoppily ever after!*

Knock knock.
Who's there?
Duxgo.
Duxgo who?
No, ducks go "quack."

What happened when the oars got married?

a. They lived happily river rafter!

What bird never needs shampoo?

a. A bald eagle!

Knock knock.
Who's there?
Alpaca.
Alpaca who?
Alpaca bag so I can leave for my trip!

How do you know if there's a stegosaurus under your couch?

a. *If your head hits the ceiling!*

Knock knock.
Who's there?
Wendy.
Wendy who?
Wendy door opens, you'll see who it is!

Would a cat know what kind of tree this is?

a. *No, but a dogwood.*

What did the hat say to the cape?

a. *"You stay back, I'll go on a head!"*

Would mistletoe make a good movie?

a. No, but Hollywood!

What do hogs do at the park?
a. They have a pignic!

Knock knock.
Who's there?
Robin.
Robin who?
Robin your house, give me all your things!

What did the shark say when it ate the comedian?

a. "That tasted funny."

Knock knock.
Who's there?
Lena.
Lena who?
Lena bit closer so you can hear me.

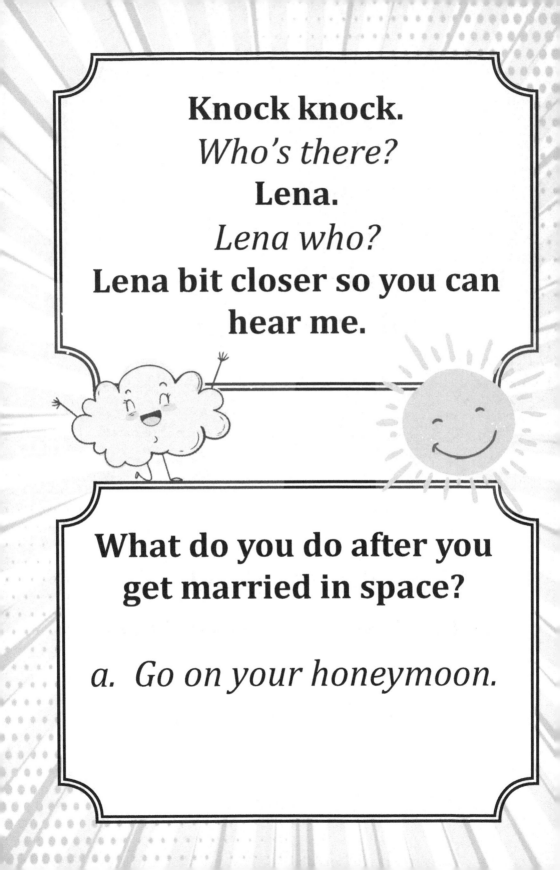

What do you do after you get married in space?

a. Go on your honeymoon.

What did the gull to the ocean after returning from a trip?

a. *"Long time no sea."*

Knock knock.
Who's there?
Kent.
Kent who?
Kent you just open the door?

Why do whales swim in salt water?

a. *Because pepper water would make them sneeze.*

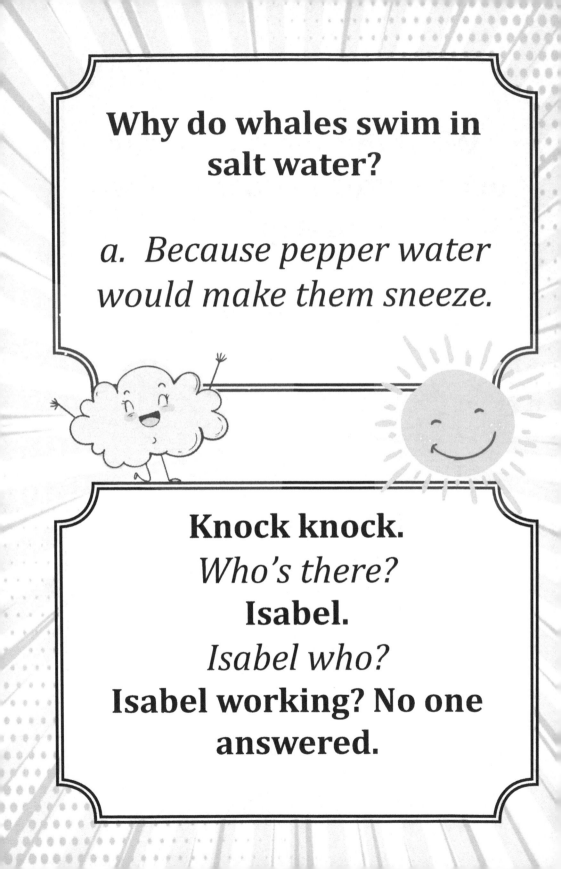

Knock knock.
Who's there?
Isabel.
Isabel who?
Isabel working? No one answered.

How do elephant hunters like their eggs?

a. Poached.

Why didn't the skeleton cross the road?

a. He had no guts!

Why did the weatherman call the vet?

a. Because it was raining cats and dogs!

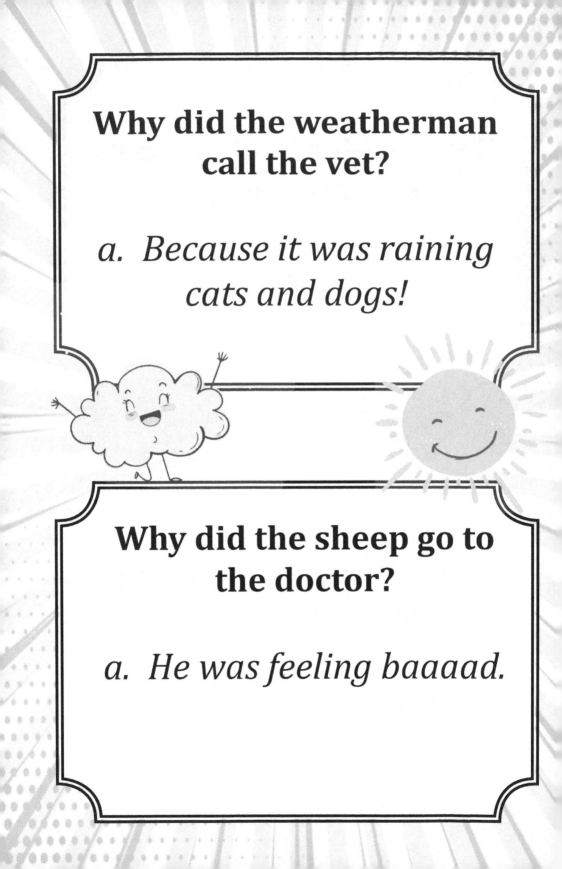

Why did the sheep go to the doctor?

a. He was feeling baaaad.

Knock knock.
Who's there?
Howard.
Howard who?
Howard you like to hang out for a little?

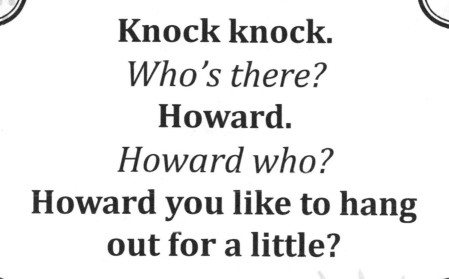

What's the best thing to put in a burrito?

a. Your teeth!

Knock knock.
Who's there?
Dwayne.
Dwayne who?
Dwayne the sink, it's starting to fill up!

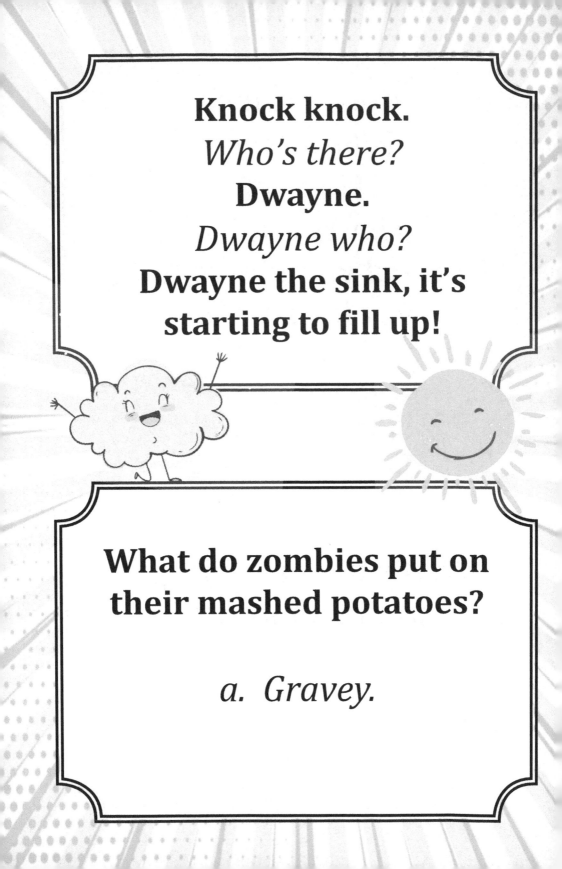

What do zombies put on their mashed potatoes?

a. Gravey.

How do you catch a ghost?

a. *Set a booby trap.*

Knock knock.
Who's there?
Claire.
Claire who?
Claire out of the way so we can come in!

Made in United States
Orlando, FL
13 October 2022

23316788R00030